Self Help 2. Motivational & Inspirational
ISBN-13: 978-0692552377
ISBN-10: 0692552375

Dedication:

May this daily dose of love help you start your day with a thankful heart and positive energy for your mind, body and spirit.

As you read the text, it is my hope that you believe that anything is possible.

Each day, embrace the words on the page and put it into practice.

I pray that you will be empowered and transformed.

Avalon

Avalon Annisette-King
Founder
Straight From Her Heart

Straight From Her Heart Ministries is an organization focused on the empowerment and uplifting of women. Originally from the island of Trinidad and Tobago, Avalon has lived in the USA for over 35 years, and is now a resident of Dallas, Texas.

She is a motivator and an inspirational speaker who is passionate about helping women who feel stuck or voiceless, discover their self-worth and purpose. As a transformational coach, she uses a unique combination of insightfulness and prayer, along with conventional coaching methods to help clients tap into their highest potential. Avalon implements a step by step plan to help clients find the clarity and direction that they seek, offering support and guidance from a place of heightened consciousness and love.

Be happy!
Fill your day with laughter,
love, and gratitude.

*Love is the most
powerful medicine.
Let's heal one another.*

I love me,
just the way that I am.

My thoughts promote continuous prosperity.

*I am doing the work
that satisfies my life.*

My beauty is the
essence of my soul.

Every day challenges help to strengthen me.

Being a blessing to others will bless you when you least expect it.

Always start your day giving thanks for God's goodness in your life.

Daily acts of kindness could change someone's life forever.

Whatever you do, make it worthy of the lovely gift of life you've been given.

Live your life fully,
with joy and gratitude!

I thank God today for His strength, His wisdom and His gift of LOVE.

Where the love of God is, there is peace. Let us love one another.

Take steps toward fulfilling the dream that God has put within you every day.

Believe in yourself
and walk by faith.

Follow your dreams.
With God all opportunities
are infinite!

Step aside, let go,
let God.

Faith and prayer will get you through any storm in your life.

*It's important to remember
God's choice of blessing
may be different from yours.*

When you obey God,
expect His Blessings.

Treat yourself like
ROYALTY!

Another lovely day has been gifted to you, enjoy every moment.

Wishing you a day of miracles.

Laughter is good for the mind, body and soul.

Live in the joy and beauty of every precious moment

Never underestimate the power of prayer.

Each day is a gift.
Give thanks for all of
your blessings.

Bless someone with your smile.

Go after what your heart longs for; those desires have been planted by God.

Appreciate your friends and family.

I am gifted, chosen and blessed.

It's a new day absolutely filled with possibilities.

Go chase your dreams.

Miracles do happen.

*Say out loud and believe it:
something good is going to
happen to me today!*

Acts of kindness are a gift from the heart.

Take time for the three R's.
Relax, Renew, and Refocus.

Don't ever give up on your dreams, no matter how big, how old, or how seemingly impossible they are.

When we set others free by our forgiveness, we truly express the love of God.

Welcome every new day. Use it joyously and brilliantly.

I trust my inner voice to guide me.

*Live in the joy and beauty
of every precious moment*

Set yourself free from any limitations through the conscious decision to forgive.

Be You –
beautiful and unique.

Give God praise for your family today.

Trust in God's power to be with you, to bless you and to make all things right.

Consciously share love with everyone you come in contact with today.

Love is the most powerful
medicine. Let's heal one
another.

Be happy!

Fill your day with laughter, love, and gratitude.

Love yourself!
Listen to the needs of
your body and your spirit.

Today is filled with beauty, peace and love.

We are all children of the Most High.
Let us treat each other with love and respect.

Today, let LOVE
be your guide.

Today, look around and see the humor in life.

Laughter lifts your spirit and brings joy to your heart. Laugh today!

May your life be filled with unlimited potential.

I am healthy strong and filled with vitality.

God has given me all the tools to be successful.

I attract abundant increase.

Learn more about the various services
that Straight From Her Heart offers

Website:
wwww.straightfromherheart.com

www.ingramcontent.com/pod-product-compliance
Lightning Source LLC
Chambersburg PA
CBHW071022040426
42443CB00007B/901